skills: transforming business

towards a better skilled and more competitive workforce

sub-editor:	Lesley Malachowski
production manager:	Lisa Robertson
design:	Halo Design
commercial director:	Ed Hicks
publishing director:	Tom Nash
chief operating officer:	Andrew Main Wilson
chairman:	Miles Templeman

Published for the Institute of Directors
and the Learning and Skills Council
by Director Publications Ltd
116 Pall Mall London SW1Y 5ED
Ⓣ 020 7766 8950 Ⓦ www.iod.com

Funded by
the Learning and
Skills Council

about the Learning and Skills Council

The Learning and Skills Council (LSC) is working to make England better skilled and more competitive. It has the challenging role of investing public money in high-quality vocational education and training to deliver the skills employers and individuals need. Our vision is that by 2010, young people and adults will have the knowledge and skills matching the best in the world and be part of a truly competitive workforce.

To achieve this aim we are committed to transforming post-16 learning and skills in England. Too many people do not have the foundation skills they need for work or to achieve the quality of life they want. Furthermore, the need to improve the skills of the workforce in order to boost productivity is one of the biggest challenges facing business.

We want to make learning truly 'demand-led'. The Employer Training Pilots make it as easy as possible for employers to identify skills gaps and understand how these can be filled through training. Apprenticeships are now at record levels. Centres of Vocational Excellence show how colleges and businesses can work together to develop flexible and responsive programmes for learners. We want to ensure this partnership approach is adopted throughout the whole further education sector and are working with them to achieve this.

Through our network of 47 local offices, the LSC has an important leadership role, providing drive and direction to the delivery of world-class learning and skills. At least 40 per cent of our local Council members are employers and they ensure that the work we do directly helps to meet the needs of business now and in the future.

CONTENTS

introduction
tackling the skills crisis ———————————————— 5
Miles Templeman, Director General, IoD

foreword
the backbone of the economy ———————————————— 7
Chris Banks, Chairman, Learning and Skills Council

1   mind the gap———————————————————— 9

2   how did we get here? ———————————————— 15

3   aligning skills to business strategy——————————— 21

4   carrying out a skills audit ———————————————— 25

5   developing a skills strategy ———————————————— 31

6   upskilling your existing workforce ——————————— 35

7   attracting new talent———————————————————— 41

8   trouble at the top? ———————————————————— 47

9   measuring progress ———————————————————— 53

10   giving as well as receiving ——————————————— 61

11   where do we go from here? ——————————————— 66

appendices———————————————————————————

This Director's Guide has been written by independent business writers Alison Coleman, Philip Hunter and Jane Simms, with additional research and information provided by the Learning and Skills Council.

Are you qualified to be a director?

EXECUTIVE DIRECTOR

FTSE 100 company wishes to appoint a Marketing Director to the board. The candidate must either be cogniscent with all aspects of company direction and hold the IoD Diploma in Company Direction or undertake the programme on appointment. All current members of the board are Chartered Directors and it is expected that the successful candidate will progress to C Dir status.

FINANCE DIRECTOR

Medium sized organisation seeks a qualified accountant who as a member of the board is also able to make a significant contribution to the overall development of the business. Accordingly, a Chartered Director is preferred, identifying a demonstrable track record of success in delivering profitable growth.

CHAIRMAN

International company requires a Chairman to lead investor relations and present to key financial institutions. The successful candidate will hold the IoD Diploma in Company Direction and be a Chartered Director, due to the high regard for these qualifications in the investment community.

NON-EXECUTIVE DIRECTOR

A major PLC is looking to expand its board with an experienced NED. The candidate must be a Chartered Director and therefore demonstrate the highest levels of strategic direction and the profile to communicate with shareholders.

CHIEF EXECUTIVE

This not for profit organisation is seeking an experienced chief executive possessing high standards of leadership and ability to guide the organisation through a period of restructuring and regional expansion. In addition, knowledge of and adherence to, sound corporate governance is essential. Only Chartered Directors will be considered for this position.

COMPANY SECRETARY

A FTSE 50 organisation seeks a company secretary who can demonstrate the experience and confidence to work with a high profile main board consisting of Chartered Directors. The successful candidate is also expected to contribute to the strategic direction of the company and be a senior team leader. Preference will be given to a Chartered Secretary who has also qualified as a Chartered Director.

These positions are fictitious but are representative of Chartered Directors and their organisations.

Chartered Director is the IoD's professional qualification for directors and receives the endorsement and support of government, regulators, the investment community, executive search agencies, the public sector and organisations including FTSE 100 companies.

tackling the skills crisis

**Miles Templeman, Director General
Institute of Directors**

The UK faces a serious skills shortage, with one in ten employees regarded as incompetent by their employers. That is the equivalent of 2.4m people undermining the productivity and competitiveness of their company.

The full scale of our skills deficiency was revealed by the Learning and Skills Council's National Employers Skills Survey (NESS) in 2003. It showed that UK businesses across all sectors are affected, from engineering and construction to healthcare and IT, and at all levels, from shop floor workers to senior managers.

Many employees do not even possess basic literacy and numeracy skills, which, according to Ernst & Young, is costing UK businesses £10bn a year. And, as the UK moves towards a value-added, skills-based economy, both individuals and employers will be faced with even more challenges.

The guide's core message is that businesses need to acknowledge the skills shortage or gaps that are constraining them and adopt a systematic approach to upskilling their workforce. As well as tackling problems internally, businesses are being called on to participate in the development of new skills initiatives. Looking to the future, businesses must ensure that further education colleges and providers can deliver training that meets their skills needs. What better way than to get more involved themselves?

But the onus isn't only on businesses, 90 per cent of whom provide training and dedicate £23.5bn to it. The government also needs to address achievement levels in schools, to raise the number of school leavers with decent qualifications and to ensure all young people leave education literate and numerate.

FACT:

Over a quarter of a million apprentices are working for business, right now.

Apprenticeships, a great idea for any business.

the backbone of the economy

**Chris Banks, chairman,
Learning and Skills Council**

Skills are the backbone of a successful economy and a measure of a nation's ability to survive in a global marketplace. Acquiring the right skills is also, quite simply, a way to improve our quality of life.

The Learning and Skills Council (LSC) exists to ensure that young people and adults in this country have the skills to match the best in the world, as part of a productive workforce. We are committed to putting the needs of employers as well as individuals at the heart of all we do. That is why I am really pleased that the Learning and Skills Council and the IoD have collaborated on this book. It is a great resource for directors of any type or size of business looking to reap the benefits of improving the skills of their workforce – whether this is increased efficiency and quality of product or simply better morale.

The National Institute of Economic and Social Research estimates that 20 per cent of the productivity gap between the UK and Germany is a result of a poorly skilled workforce. With 5.2m adults in this country unable to read or write properly and 15m with low basic numeracy, it is not surprising that we lag behind many of our European neighbours.

There is a huge amount of work going on within the further education sector to ensure that it is able to deliver the right kind of training for business. Increasingly colleges and work-based learning providers are offering more flexible forms of training, for example, evening courses for employees unable to spare the time from work or courses held at an organisation's premises.

I am really keen to hear your views about this book and indeed, your views on how colleges and other training providers can deliver for you. Please do e-mail me at: skills@lsc.gov.uk.

Within this guide, you will find a wide range of advice and ideas about skills and staff development. A skilled workforce underpins everything in business and it is worth taking the time to ensure that yours is one of the best.

mind the gap

Alison Coleman explores the impact of the current skills shortage on individuals, businesses, and the competitiveness of the UK economy

One of the biggest challenges facing UK industry today is the shortage of skilled workers. It is an issue that cuts right across the economy, affecting all areas from engineering and construction to healthcare and IT, and all levels of employment, from shop floor workers to senior management.

Despite the UK workforce being better qualified than ever before, persistent skills gaps remain. Skills gaps refer to deficiencies in an existing workforce, whereas the term 'skills shortage' relates to the inability to recruit staff with requisite skills. There are currently pockets of acute skills shortages in sectors such as construction, hospitality and transport, although in terms of existing employees skills gaps are more common than skills shortages.

EXECUTIVE SUMMARY

- ☐ overcoming the skills shortage crisis is critical for both individual employers and the competitiveness of the UK economy
- ☐ lack of basic skills is costing UK business £10bn a year
- ☐ UK businesses are lagging behind those in US, France and Germany in terms of productivity
- ☐ without basic skills, individuals can get stuck in a low pay/no pay cycle

obstacles to learning

It isn't that companies and individuals in the UK are failing to invest in training and development, but rather that market issues and other barriers often limit that investment. Many feel that the returns on development are uncertain or only become apparent in the long term. But the impact is felt at all levels, by industry, by businesses and by the individual.

POOR LEVELS OF PARTICIPATION

The UK is the world's fourth biggest economy, yet every day 3.5m people go to work who can't read well. The impact of such skills deficiencies is greatest on customer services, the loss of business to competitors, and delays to the development of new products or services.

Business as Usual, a recent survey by the National Institute for Adult Continuing Education (NIACE), confirms the need to tackle the falling number of adults who to continue to participate in formal learning.

The survey reveals that the number of adults reporting they are currently learning (19 per cent) is the lowest of any year since 1996, when it was four per cent higher.

In addition, the survey finds that higher paid workers showed a marked increase in participation in the late nineties, although this has now tailed off. While the number of young people participating in learning continues to grow, participation among the poorest sectors of society has declined.

On the positive side, the NIACE survey also shows that 80 per cent of 17-19-year-olds and 62 per cent of 20-24-year-olds are current or recent learners. This could be seen as proof that the widening participation agenda is being tackled at source and that young people are developing a new and more positive approach to learning. But with 36 per cent of adults saying they have not participated in learning since leaving full-time education, there is considerable work to be done.

Director of NIACE Alan Tuckett says: "The jobs that will need to be done over the next ten years cannot be filled just by the young people coming into the job market. During this period, we will also see more migration of minorities, women, and older people who cannot afford to retire. These are the people who must be equipped with the right skills."

There are signs of progress, however, with employers participating in the LSC-led Employer Training Pilots (ETPs) – a tailored and more flexible way of diagnosing and meeting employers skills needs – have recorded a 90 per cent satisfaction response.

The Learning and Skills Council's 'Skills in England' research report 2003 highlights evidence suggesting that part of the explanation for the UK's poor productivity performance compared with its international competitors lies in its poor workforce skills. The report found that more than one in five employers (22 per cent) said that their workforce's skills were not up to scratch. This figure has a direct impact on the bottom line for a third of employers, who said that it resulted in higher operating costs, orders being lost and new product development being delayed.

Over a fifth of these employers said they lost orders as a result, with quality and customer service significantly affected. A fifth of job vacancies – some

135,000 – are also going unfilled due to skill shortages, employers said, and they were losing business to competitors as a result.

CBI data published in late 2003 showed that one in three companies are exporting jobs overseas, with a further four in 10 feeling pressure to do so. A quarter of those polled cited labour skills as a key factor in their decision to relocate abroad. This is a particular problem for small firms focused on maintaining short-term cash flow.

having a proper strategy

Another issue is that many employers do not have a proper strategy in place that sets out what courses would make a difference to individual performance; how and when to implement the training; and the importance of reviewing its impact. Estimates vary on the amount invested by employers in upskilling adults, but it could be as much as £23bn a year.

The competitive strategy of many firms is based on a low cost/low added value approach. In some instances this perpetuates what is known as a low skill/low wage equilibrium in which neither employees nor employers demand higher levels of skills.

Pressures on time and the bottom line are also obstacles to participation for some individuals and firms. Untapping the motivation in individuals with low skills is another critical challenge.

Tackling basic skills such as literacy and numeracy is a top priority. Without them individuals cannot start to develop a career path and may find themselves trapped in a low pay/no pay cycle.

The real impact on business becomes evident when such people are asked to go beyond the familiar. Many suffer from a lack of confidence and find it difficult to attempt to improve basic communication skills or pursue vocational qualifications. They will avoid more demanding roles or taking on extra responsibility within their existing role. As a consequence their skills status remains static, as does their potential earning power and productivity.

COST TO BUSINESS

Research from Ernst & Young has put losses through lack of basic skills as high as £10bn a year. It states that a typical business with 50 employees loses £165,000 a year through lack of basic skills.

Of equal concern is that UK labour productivity currently lags behind that of other major industrialised countries. The research suggests there are a number of reasons for this, including a comparatively poor level of skills and the interaction between low skills and low investment. Significantly, output per hour worked is around 30 per cent higher in the US, France and Germany than in the UK. Up to a fifth of this productivity gap with Germany and France is as a direct result of lower skills levels in the UK.

While eight out of ten UK employers are addressing skills deficiencies – and spending some £4.5bn on training in the process - only half of employees are benefiting. Moreover, four out of ten employers had provided no training at all for their employees in the 12 months prior to the survey.

The benefits to employers of upskilling their workforce are numerous. There are often very simple benefits such as fewer accidents because people are able to read the health and safety notices.

level 2 qualifications and beyond

The UK government's long-term aim is that all adults should have the opportunity to achieve a Level 2 qualification (equal to five A-C GCSEs or their vocational equivalent). Gaining skills at Level 2 allows individuals to make progress at work: access to better training and possibly promotion increases once individuals get on the development ladder. For those who achieve qualifications above Level 2, the returns provide a greater incentive to both them and their employers to invest further in skills. This is crucial for the employee because personal benefits such as better earnings are still relatively low up to a Level 2 qualification.

The big challenge, therefore, is to build a stable and substantial skills base that will support a sustainable enterprise environment.

A highly skilled workforce is more innovative and much better able to adapt to the demands of a changing economy. It has been shown that businesses with higher productivity are more likely to have a higher proportion of skilled workers.

If the UK is to raise its game on skills, it needs to address the following core issues:

- ☐ ensuring that more young people leave the education system equipped for employment, with basic skills, good qualifications and a positive attitude

- ☐ reducing the number of adults in the workforce without a Level 2 qualification to ensure everyone has the skills essential for employment

- ☐ enabling businesses to raise their performance through flexible cost-effective training that is tailored to their needs

According to findings from the LSC's National Employers Skills Survey (NESS), which was carried out in 2003, businesses must also have access to information on what support is available to meet their needs, what funding they can access, and better signposting of how different skills and training organisations and initiatives fit together.

SO YOU'RE THE BIG CHEESE. YOU'VE MATURED INTO A FINE SPECIMEN. YOU THINK YOU CAN'T BE IMPROVED UPON.

WELL THAT STINKS. PERHAPS YOU'RE JUST GOING MOULDY.

WE MEAN BUSINESS

'e're sniffing out all the bosses out there. Incredibly, some them aren't even aware of the major challenge currently ing the UK. Productivity is in trouble. It's falling way behind.

hile countries like Germany, the US, Canada and France ofit from their lifelong commitment to learning in the rkplace, the UK's managers for the most part, don't lise that in comparison, our productivity is low.

d it's now widely recognised that one of the major causes the UK's low productivity levels is a shortfall in leadership d management skills.

, there's room for improvement.

A lack of management expertise has a knock on effect on the workforce too. If bosses aren't developing their own skills, how can they competently steer the rest of their organisation?

They can't. That's where we come in. The Skills for Business network is made up of Sector Skills Councils (SSCs), which are led by employers, and bring together industry leaders, trade unionists and the government to address the UK's skills issues.

For the first time, employers will have the voice and the power to positively affect skills levels. By working with training and education providers to develop products and services that meet their needs, employers can make sure their vision becomes a reality.

skills
FOR BUSINESS

isit www.skillsforbusiness.org.uk and extend your sell-by date

how did we get here?

Alison Coleman highlights some of the key findings of the Learning and Skills Council's major survey on the importance of the UK's skills shortage, and pinpoints the origins of the current crisis

The scale of the UK's current skills shortages – which exist because of a lack of skilled candidates to do a job – was highlighted last year, with the publication of the annual National Employers Skills Survey (NESS) by the Learning and Skills Council (LSC), the organisation that exists to make England better skilled and more competitive. The survey was the largest ever conducted into employers and the skills of their workforce. Its findings reveal that the cause of the crisis is, in part, a legacy of poor education that has left thousands of working adults without a good grounding in basic skills such as numeracy and literacy.

However, the greater legacy is the UK's poor track record in providing work-based training to people beyond their early to mid-thirties. David Way, director of skills at the LSC, says: "For the first time we could see quite clearly where the skills gaps were and, more importantly, the effect they have on industry, both now and in the future. One of the most alarming statistics was that 80 per cent of new jobs over the next 10 years will require people with Level 3 and 4 qualifications and above. That is an issue that has to be tackled now, not in 10 years' time."

EXECUTIVE SUMMARY

- ☐ one in five employers believe that their workforce's skills are inadequate
- ☐ however, many may be unaware of their employee's poor level of numeracy and literacy
- ☐ poor leadership skills are a major obstacle to improving the UK's economic performance

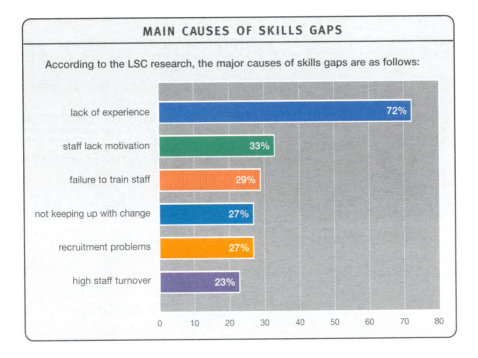

MAIN CAUSES OF SKILLS GAPS

According to the LSC research, the major causes of skills gaps are as follows:

- lack of experience — 72%
- staff lack motivation — 33%
- failure to train staff — 29%
- not keeping up with change — 27%
- recruitment problems — 27%
- high staff turnover — 23%

NESS was conducted among 72,100 employers. It makes for stark reading, revealing that more than one in 10 workers (11 per cent) are considered to be incompetent by their employers – the equivalent of 2.4m people. While employers said that incompetence was largely due to inexperience, a significant number of skills gaps were attributed to a 'lack of motivation' (33 per cent) and 'not keeping up with change' (27 per cent).

impact on the bottom line

More than one in five employers (22 per cent) said their workforce's skills were not up to scratch. This figure has a direct impact on the bottom line for a third of employers, who said that it resulted in higher operating costs, orders being lost and new product development being delayed. Small businesses are the most likely to lose orders because of a lack of skilled staff.

Over a fifth of employers also said that quality and customer service are significantly affected.

losing out to competitors

A further finding of the survey is that a fifth of job vacancies – some 135,000 – are going unfilled due to skills shortages. Employers also said that they were losing business to competitors as a result.

Some of the worst skills shortages are found in the wood and paper industry, where 65 per cent of vacancies are not filled, followed by construction (38 per cent) and the motor vehicles and transport equipment industry (35 per cent).

By area, the West Midlands experienced the highest proportion of skills short-age vacancies (24 per cent), but many other areas fared little better. London has the worst training record, with four in 10 employers providing no instruction.

Employer skills needs have been identified and met through sector-based training in more than 30 occupational groups and the LSC's investment of

INVESTING IN THE FUTURE

Schemes such as Apprenticeships (see chapter 7) have a key role to play in giving young people the skills they need to do the job to the high standards employers require. Fuji Film Electronic Imaging specialises in making professional photo imaging and pre-press machines that are distributed across the Americas, Asia Pacific and Europe.

The Peterborough plant faces the same recruitment challenge as the rest of the manufac-turing industry: recruiting good engineers. When Chris Medlock, one of their newest recruits, showed real potential, Fuji took the step of approaching a local training provider and enrolling Chris on an NVQ within a Modern Apprenticeship in Engineering.

After this initial success, Fuji's Peterborough plant is now looking to recruit more Apprentices to help feed their longer-term need for senior engineers. Such a move will involve making a 15-year investment in each individual.

Nigel Birch, head of engineering, says: "In our market it is important that we invest in the right people and foster a culture of continuous change if we are to adapt to emerging technologies. Apprenticeships are likely to become an important part of our investment in the future.

"Manufacturing our products requires technical understanding and accuracy. Apprentice-ships have already proven valuable in helping us to acquire the breadth and depth of skills we need. We're confident it will continue to enable us to recruit candidates of a high calibre who are also highly motivated people."

over £20m in the past year. Together with employer contributions, this has helped train some 27,000 additional adults. Many are progressing to Level 3 qualifications and beyond, supporting the aim set out in the Skills Strategy White Paper.

the value of soft skills

Other key areas in which employees are viewed as being less than proficient, sector-wide, include soft skills such as communication, customer handling, team working and problem solving. However, in reality, engineers benefit from having 'soft' skills, such as project management and communication skills just as much as front-of-house retail staff.

Nevertheless, employers also share some of the blame for failing to help staff acquire the skills and motivation needed to carry out their jobs efficiently. Indeed, almost a third of employers admitted that their own failure to train staff was contributing to skills-related problems.

true picture hidden from sight

But, at a more basic level, many businesses may not realise that some of their employees have problems with literacy and numeracy. Most adults with poor literacy or numeracy skills find ways to 'get by' and are adept at hiding the fact from others.

However, it is crucial that such skills gaps come to light since these basic skills are just as important as more specialised skills, without them people lack confidence and won't progress.

David Way says: "A lot of work is being done at local level to address basic skills shortages, through partnerships between local authorities, community and voluntary groups and local colleges and providers.

"People are often daunted by the prospect of travelling to a new college or a large formal institution, but they will put their faith and trust in a local organisation. They get a taste of learning, enjoy it, and go on to do something else. These may only be small steps, but a vital part of the bigger picture."

PUBLIC SECTOR TRAINING PROVISION

Business Link
Offers advice and support services to businesses
www.businesslink.gov.uk

Education and Learning in Wales (ELWa)
Provides the same service in Wales.
www.elwa.ac.uk

JobCentre Plus
Offers a fully integrated work and benefit services, including access to skills training.
www.jobcentreplus.gov.uk

learndirect
A government-sponsored initiative for flexible learning. Much of the training is delivered online.
www.learndirect.co.uk

The Learning and Skills Council (LSC)
The LSC exists to make England better skilled and more competitive. It is responsible for planning and funding high-quality vocational education and training for everyone with the aim to improve the skills of England's young people and adults to world-class standards.
www.lsc.gov.uk

Regional Development Agencies
These are non-departmental public bodies whose primary role is as strategic drivers of regional economic development in their region. This includes ensuring the development of a regional skills action plan to ensure that skills training matches the needs of the labour market.
www.englandsrdas.com

The Sector Skills Councils (SSCs)
Government-licensed but independent organisations that bring together employers, trade unions and professional bodies. Their aim is to identify and tackle skills shortages and gaps by sector, and to direct people to approved training courses.
www.ssda.org.uk

Union Learning Fund
Provides funding to help trade unions to encourage greater take-up of learning at work.
www.unionlearningfund.org.uk

Skills needs can also be met by courses run through local community schools, FE colleges, and universities

lack of leadership skills

At a more senior level, the shortage of appropriate and practical leadership skills among UK managers is also acknowledged as a serious obstacle to improved economic performance. In spite of widespread management education, many business schools and training providers have been criticised for being too inflexible and not being prepared to tailor courses for individual companies or managers.

But it isn't all bad news. Government figures released in July 2004 on international skills comparisons indicate that the UK is starting to close the gap with its major competitors at the intermediate and technician skill levels, which are vital for productivity.

Analysis of changes in skills levels in the UK, US, France, Germany and Singapore between 1994 and 2003, shows that the UK had the highest growth rate for qualifications at Level 2 (equivalent to five GSCEs grades A-C) and above. The UK is also narrowing the gap with Germany and the US at Level 3 (A-level equivalent) and is already ahead of all the other countries except the US at Level 4 (degree level) and above. Nonetheless, the report does highlight the large gap that still needs to be closed if the UK is to compete well with the major economic powers.

"On a global level, there is so much change, complexity and competition," says David Way. "It is vital that directors and managers understand the value and necessity of constantly replenishing skills – both for themselves and their staff – because it is only through that process that they are going to stay ahead."

aligning skills to business strategy

A skills strategy needs to relate directly to a company's business strategy and be designed to help realise future objectives, says Alison Coleman

Employee skills are still seen by many companies as relating to soft skills rather than something that is fundamental to business development and success.

However, findings from the Learning and Skills Council's National Employment and Skills Survey 2003 indicate that skills shortages – ie. difficulty in recruiting people with the right skills – have a very direct impact on business. Almost half of employers with 'skills shortage vacancies' said they were losing business to competitors as a result of their lack of skilled workers.

Skills gaps within employers' existing work-forces are also a major problem (see chapter 2). And, recruitment problems are also putting the country's innovation under threat. For example, 36 per cent of employers with vacancies they were unable to fill said they had to delay developing new products as a result.

Sarah Bentley, LSC skills policy manager, says: "Until recently, it is true to say that skills were the last thing that many business

EXECUTIVE SUMMARY

- ☐ a skilled and flexible workforce is central to a business's success
- ☐ a skills strategy must be shaped by the business strategy
- ☐ because businesses are continually changing the process of auditing, planning, implementing and reviewing skills needs is ongoing
- ☐ there are a number of initiatives that can support businesses in their efforts to train and develop their workforce

PEOPLE PARTNERSHIP

The John Lewis Partnership is famous for its employee-owned corporate structure that puts its people at the heart of its business strategy. Chairman Sir Stuart Hampson says, "If you focus on your staff as the fundamental drivers of success then you will out-perform your competitors."

This is backed up by the company's investment in staff training and development, which includes, customer service training, IT skills training, one to one help if English is a second language or staff are dyslexic, and opportunities to gain National Vocational Qualifications.

All JLP branches have a learning centre, with books, videos, tapes, CD ROMs on a whole host of subjects. There are training resources for specific company initiatives, plus a whole series of courses for managers on subjects such as leadership and change management

The company also liaises with SkillSmart, the SSC for the retail sector, on how best to provide training for staff, and is involved with the Prince's Trust.

"Companies often say they treat their staff as assets, but then do nothing about it," says Hampson. "Our first principle is that our main purpose is the happiness of our members and we don't take that lightly."

owners worried about. They were focused on getting out there, selling their products, increasing market share and profits, and really didn't make the connection between all of these objectives and a skilled workforce. That is changing and there is a growing realisation among businesses that investing in people does impact on the bottom line."

where do we want to be?

So, before companies can begin work on skills development, they need to assess their business strategy. Only when the business strategy has been clearly defined, and the business knows where it wants to be can it begin to analyse its skills requirements and any possible deficiencies. (The process of aligning skills to business strategy is covered in chapter 4.)

"It is healthy for a business to take a step back, especially where there may have been some problem areas, such as falling sales. A business owner may have put this down to changing markets or economic factors, where in fact it may be a gap in employee sales skills," says Bentley.

Having acknowledged the direct link between skills and business strategy, business owners must also accept that aligning the two is an ongoing process. The business strategy will change over time, as a result of growth and diversification and external factors such as new legislation. Skills needs should be continually reviewed and updated to keep pace with such change. Furthermore, employers need to recognise that those employees with the skills that make up the core competencies of the business may decide to leave. Clearly, recruitment and retention of staff will impact on, and be impacted by, a company's skills strategy.

where next?

In 2003, the government launched its Skills Strategy to maximise the contribution of skills to raising productivity, economic competitiveness and sustainable employment in the UK. The LSC has a range of initiatives to help businesses develop a skilled workforce and, more specifically, achieve key business objectives, such as retaining staff, reducing costs and increasing profits.

Several of these initiatives are aimed at giving every individual a strong foundation in skills and to make it easier for businesses to reskill their workforce. These include Employer Training Pilots (ETPs) and the Centres of Vocational Excellence (CoVEs).

One programme that has been successful in changing employer attitudes to long-term staff development is Investors in People (IiP). By 2006 more than 40,000 companies will have achieved the IiP Standard. Its effectiveness lies in its simplicity. As a business tool it can illustrate exactly where a business is going.

Ruth Spellman, chief executive of Investors in People UK, says: "The real success of IiP is in the way it encourages the change of mindset that is required for real long-term commitment to investment in staff development. Businesses have to see the potential benefits to business for themselves, and increasingly they are. As an agency we can lead the way and provide the support, but ultimately it is the company that has to achieve IiP, and because they are paying for it, they know that if they don't get a return on their investment, they can't do it tomorrow."

The IiP recently launched a new scheme, funded by the treasury, to encourage more small firms to achieve IiP, through heavily subsidised advice and support.

But the link between business and skills applies to all types and sizes of employer, in all industry sectors.

Taking a demand-led approach means training must respond to a specific employer need or skill gap and be delivered in a way that fits with the needs of the business – at the right time and in the right place, often outside the traditional office hours of nine to five. The employer should feel very much in the driving seat, being able to influence the training to get exactly what they need to make a difference to the bottom line.

Transforming the learning system to meet demand is the key to unlocking productivity increases needed to match and pass our economic competitors.

Skills shortages can undermine any organisation's progress towards its goals. However, with an effective development plan in place, businesses have an infra-structure for growth that can help in developing their existing employees and attracting new ones.

carrying out a
skills audit

A skills audit can help you determine whether your workforce has the necessary skills to meet the company's current objectives and ambitions for the future, says Alison Coleman

Skills gaps occur when an employer recognises that some staff are not fully capable of meeting the requirements of their job. To what extent the lack of a particular skill or set of skills matters will depend on the specific objectives of the business. Indeed, two organisations, whose workers possess identical skills, may have a different view as to whether or not they have a skills gap.

However, too often businesses only notice a skills gap at a stage where such a deficiency is critical. It would be far better to have advance notice of such weaknesses and time to take remedial steps.

How does an employer know if they've got a problem? A skills audit can help employers to:

☐ identify existing skills

☐ identify what further skills are needed to carry out existing business strategy more effectively

☐ plan, develop and improve the skills and knowledge needed for the future

In order for the exercise to be effective, those conducting it will need to have an in-depth practical knowledge of the business. However, more importantly, they need to be able to translate business objectives into resource requirements. For

EXECUTIVE SUMMARY

☐ smaller firms may benefit from calling in an expert to carry out the audit

☐ distinguishing between skills needs and skills wants is important

☐ once skills needs have been identified, they must be prioritised

☐ a skills audit can help to map the company's future

owner managers, in particular, the critical question is: do they have the skills to carry out these audits themselves? Tricia Scott, the Learning and Skills Council's skills policy manager, says: "It really depends on the size and type of company. A skills audit is essentially an alignment of skills with business objectives, and the one person who knows this better than anyone else is the owner."

For example, in companies with less than 10 employees a skills audit should not present a major problem for the owner. Scott says: "Given time, a manager with a reasonable level of confidence at problem solving would be able to do it." However, while a business may know what net result they need, they may not be able to translate that into the language of skills and competencies. In such instances, a business adviser may be able to help, but it must be the right adviser. "Ideally it should be someone with expertise in your particular sector and the best route to finding them is generally through trade associations and networks," says Scott.

working within a framework

So, what does a skills audit involve? There are generic skills categories that can be audited, that will feature to a greater or lesser degree in all businesses, and there will be more specialised – perhaps technical or vocational – skills requirements.

Training and development needs can also be identified at different levels:

- [ ] organisational – focusing on needs against business strategy and goals

- [ ] departmental – where bespoke solutions for specific departments or teams need to be assessed

- [ ] occupational – at this level training and development is closely associated with the needs of the individual's job role

Within these areas, more specific skills can be assessed, such as:

- [ ] management – how well do management personnel, including the owner/manager, motivate and get the best out of their employees?

- [ ] finance – how well-organised are the company records and documents? This is just as crucial to monitoring performance as it is for meeting tax and VAT requirements.

- ☐ customer service – now seen as a key skill by many employers, but how good are employees at dealing with customer enquiries, or complaints? Are they competent enough to solve customer issues through to resolution?

- ☐ IT – Assessment of current systems already in place and whether staff are fully conversant with all the programmes and equipment needed to do their own job, as well as fill in for other jobs when required? Do systems need upgrading, and if so, will additional staff training be required?

- ☐ sales and marketing – how effective is the sales team? How good are they at promoting the business and sourcing potential clients?

formal qualifications are not always necessary

One common misconception by business owners is that qualifications are the panacea to skills shortages and skills gaps. However, while qualifications provide evidence of competence, in many cases, a skills gap may only need a 'bite-sized' piece of knowledge to be filled at any one point in time.

On the other hand, using training and development to enable employees to gain formal qualifications can be highly significant in raising staff motivation.

mandatory training requirements

Once aligned with the business strategy, a skills audit may identify a whole range of skills needs which should be prioritised and sequenced into immediate and future needs. This enables them to be managed within the constraints of organisational budget.

Industries such as construction and healthcare may also be subject to additional legislative requirements relating to health and safety.

Security, too, is currently going through mandatory regulation that will affect the training and qualifications needed by employees, regardless of the specific skills gaps of the individual business. In such cases, these basic standards should be prioritised over and above any of the other training needs of the business.

RAISING THE BAR ON SKILLS DEVELOPMENT

Builders merchant Penlaw and Co, based in Wickford, undertook a skills audit to identify skills gaps among its 26-strong workforce in anticipation of its expansion plans.

The company wanted to expand into the drywall market and open five new premises. Co-owner Paul Scott organised a skills audit to ensure they were implementing a sufficiently flexible, accessible and manageable training programme for the planned growth.

The firm had already identified skills gaps through job discussion interviews and drawn up a plan to meet potential training requirements. Previously the company had provided a basic form of training to employees relating to its own products, but found the results to be hit and miss.

Penlaw signed up for an Employer Training Pilot programme, a LSC initiative that gives small businesses access to a pot of money to help train their staff and provides compensation for the time their employees take off work to train. The company's staff were trained in basic maths and English, and customer services – the latter being key to staff development as it gave a general grounding and awareness of its importance to the business.

continual process

Addressing skills needs shouldn't stop with the skills audit. "If a company is addressing the issue from the top down it should be feeding the findings and the solution into the whole performance review process," says Scott.

Theoretically, this should be more straightforward in a smaller business, where the owner has a clear overview of the skills picture, on an ongoing basis. This should make it easier to ensure that the skills monitoring and review process is evident throughout the company. However, in reality, time is a scarce resource for many owners of smaller companies, who have to commit much of their time to fire fighting at ground level leaving them with scant opportunity to gain an overview.

In larger companies, it falls to the middle managers to communicate problem areas to the decision makers. With every line manager needing to be aware of the importance of keeping skills aligned with business, that in itself may prove to be a skills gap that needs to be addressed.

It may be easier for businesses to source training provision using the services of a broker, whose role it is to work with employers and find the course and funding that is most appropriate for their requirements.

Broker services are provided by a number of organisations, including local colleges, independent organisations, and government-funded bodies such as the Learning and Skills Council and Business Link.

At Business Link Derbyshire, workforce development manager Linda Pearson says: "We listen, diagnose, provide information, and then broker the company's training requirements. This service is very much in demand, and has become more so recently as the issue of skills shortages is brought more into focus."

The service is free, and provided across the Business Link network.

Employers need to have a clear idea of where they want to be in two, five or 10 years time and need to know what that future workforce will look like. For many a skills audit is the logical place to start.

Powering the nation's skills

Local colleges are the biggest force in the UK tackling the nation's skills shortages.

In England alone, 400 colleges deliver education and training to 3.5 million adults. They deliver more than half the annual total of vocational qualifications into the economy. Your local college will have links with over 500 local firms.

Cornwall College has 60,000 adults - one quarter of the county's workforce – in education and training

Telford College provides tailored on-site training for 8,000 employees in hundreds of local companies

Logistics North West brings together 6 colleges to meet the national demand for 100,000 extra HGV drivers by 2010

New College, Swindon works with customers such as Honda and Zurich Financial Services to deliver skills ranging from IT management to work-based English and Maths.

Local colleges work with business communities to build the pool of skills you need now and in the future

AoC Workforce Development 01244 400 005

developing a skills strategy

Alison Coleman outlines some of the key issues that companies should cover when assembling a skills strategy

Having identified where skills shortages or gaps are in the workforce, the real challenge facing employers is addressing them. The approach they take must not only make an impact on skills shortfalls, it must also lend itself to the long-term development of the workforce and dovetail with the business strategy.

Developing a skills strategy requires the same focus as developing a business strategy. With the information gleaned from the skills audit, business owners need to implement a long-term programme of training and development for every member of the workforce.

The strategy must be flexible enough to withstand the demands of change, whether this comes about through a move into new markets or a merger.

EXECUTIVE SUMMARY

- [ ] a skills strategy must cover all areas of staff development
- [ ] flexibility is key as the strategy will have to adapt the business changes
- [ ] tracking who has what skills at any one time is important
- [ ] help is at hand from Sector Skills Councils (SSCs)

Professor Mike Campbell, director of strategy and research at the Sector Skills Development Agency (SSDA), says: "Business owners are known to take a reactive approach to training requirements, for example, only responding when there are new recruits or specific problems to address. A skills strategy must encompass all areas of staff development.

"As well as developing functional or technical skills, a sizeable component of the strategy should be dedicated to transferable skills. These can be the key to a company's competitive advantage."

These include oral and written communication skills, as well as intermediate and high-level computing skills. Enterprise skills, which enable people to be creative or good at problem solving can also be of huge value to a business. "These individual skills areas must be brought together and linked to a central strategy. Good management and leadership skills here are absolutely critical," says Campbell.

For many companies, IT is an obvious place to start, as skills needs frequently extend throughout the whole organisation. The following statistics on IT skills and users come from e-skills UK, the sector skills council for the IT industry, and highlight how prevalent the need for good IT skills is:

- [ ] in a workforce of 28m people, around 21m use IT in their jobs
- [ ] nine out of 10 new jobs require IT skills
- [ ] around 75 per cent of British companies claim employee time is wasted through a lack of computing skills
- [ ] under trained IT users are six times more likely to require IT support than adequately trained users

Karen Price, chief executive of e-skills UK, says: "We are looking at a huge need by a huge workforce. In terms of the lower end of the basic skills gap there is evidence that IT is one of the things that people are keenest to learn, so this can act as a lead in for employers to engage people in other training."

In order for a skills strategy to be effective, employers must also have some means of identifying and tracking individual skills and competencies at any one time. Given the complex and fragmented IT professional and end-user training industry, this is no small task.

The e-skills passport is a web-based tool that people can use to assess themselves and then self select, or have their employer select, a pre-set training profile.

"It makes the whole skills identification process much simpler and quicker," says Price. "In the past a person's CV may have stated that they were strong in a particular area of IT, or had some obscure qualification, without anyone really knowing what it meant.

"The e-skills passport takes it right back to basics and provides the employer with an instant overview of the workforce's IT skills level. It also signposts them to what training is appropriate and what is available, either from public or private training providers."

The e-skills passport is just one example of how a skills strategy can be assembled with help from the relevant sector skills council. SSCs, as well as other public and private training providers, can help businesses take steps towards developing an overall skills strategy that will boost productivity and drive the business forward. (See case study below for an example of how SSCs can work in partnership with the Learning and Skills Council and employers.)

See chapter 2 for a list of public training providers. For details on training colleges in your area, contact the education department of your local education authority.

THE SKILLS AT WORK PROGRAMME

There has been a marked change from supply-led to demand-led workforce development programmes, as evidenced by the work Leicester College is undertaking with local businesses as part of the Skills at Work programme.

Skills at Work is a skills development programme run by Leicestershire Learning and Skills Council (LSC), which offers employers across all sectors up to 35 hours' compensation for time spent by staff learning new skills. In addition, it provides free or low-cost training tailored to the needs of individuals.

Walkers Midshires, a food manufacturing specialist based in Leicester, identified a specific requirement for health and safety training for a large number of its workforce. Through Skills at Work funding, Leicester College worked with the company on a staff development programme with a specific focus on health and safety.

Tracy Billingham, personnel development manager at Walkers Midshires, said: "Every three years we refresh our health and safety training, but this time we changed from our usual training scheme. By using Skills at Work, we have been able to put 12 of our staff through the Chartered Institute of Environmental Health training programme.

"The response of those taking part in Skills at Work has been excellent. The increase in staff motivation is clear for all to see, so we'll definitely be putting another 12 people through the same training next year."

A POLISHED PERFORMANCE

In 2002 the LSC developed a pilot with ASSETT SKILLS, the Sector Skills Council for property services, housing, cleaning services and facilities management, and other key stakeholders. The main objective was to value and qualify cleaning staff who, traditionally, have had limited opportunities to train and acquire qualifications or progress to Level 2.

Many of the cleaning staff had basic skills needs. The pilot provided them with the opportunity to update these by delivering communication and literacy skills as part of their cleaning NVQ.

The Cleaning Sector Pilot was carried out in six areas in partnership with FE colleges. Training providers recruited learners in their areas and developed a learning route to meet the needs of the learner and employer. Meanwhile, the colleges provided a combination of group learning sessions, that were supplemented with individual activity and one-to-one sessions. Activities were conducted at times that suited the employer and learner, including evenings and weekends.

Of the 499 learners who signed up for the pilot, 41 per cent went on to work towards a NVQ Level 2. Of these 206, 178 (86 per cent) completed their training and achieved their qualification by the end of March 2004. As part of their training, the cleaners learned what the ideal ratio of detergent to water was. This has had a direct and positive impact on their businesses' bottom line. The pilot also demonstrated that staff who are provided with an opportunity to train are more likely to remain with their employer.

upskilling your existing workforce

There are a number of government-backed schemes that provide financial support to companies for training. Alison Coleman offers some pointers

All skills needs should be derived from business issues. Once a skills strategy has been developed, businesses need access to the resources that will help them maintain momentum and to meet their skills requirements.

Some businesses may discover that certain skills they need are already available in-house. For example, senior employees in the sales and marketing department may be able to mentor and develop customer service skills among more junior employees. Many businesses use shadowing techniques, where new members of staff spend the early part of their employment watching a more experienced member of staff.

EXECUTIVE SUMMARY

- ☐ some skills gaps can be filled informally, through mentoring and shadowing
- ☐ basic skills training can act as a catalyst for getting people back into training

But other skills may necessitate a more formal approach, in which case, the challenge for employers is finding the right training and funding it. One source of funding and support is the Employer Training Pilots. Launched in 2002 by the LSC, they are designed to help employers train their staff, improve productivity and boost employee career prospects. Employers, with the help of advisers or brokers, identify the skills gaps among their workforce and decide what training they would like them to receive (see chapter 4). The LSC introduces them to local training companies that can plug the gap.

TOP TO BOTTOM TRAINING

Advanced Roofing and Flooring is a small business based in Ilkeston, Derbyshire. The company provides a range of services including leak detection, repair and refurbishing work. Gordon Harris, managing director and part owner of the company, met with a Learning and Skills Council (LSC) advisor who carried out a skills needs analysis.

They decided that 18 of the 27 employees would benefit from basic skills training. Site workers and office staff would work towards Level 2 NVQs over a period of 10-11 months. The employers were entitled to 35 hours' wage compensation through ETP-funding.

South East Derbyshire College and Sarnafil, a specialist industry training provider, trained office-based employees in team building, ICT, leadership and management skills to NVQ Level 2. Sarnafil trained the roofing technicians on site in the use of waterproofing membranes.

Gordon Harris says it was not only the employees who fitted the criteria for participation in the ETP who benefited. 'The beauty was that although we didn't all fit the profile, it expanded the impact of our small training budget, and since some started doing an NVQ, now everyone is doing one. I'm doing an NVQ Level 4 in management.

"It's got us into the training loop. Our operations director has just completed a course. Every time he comes back from a course with something that has enthused him and it's changed him as a manager."

David Greer, national project manager for ETPs, says: "There is a history of training in this country, where if you are qualified and skilled you get many more training opportunities than if you are not. The pilots offer employers a range of incentives to overcome those barriers of cost and time in improving skills and helping to drive businesses up the value chain."

ETPs benefit businesses and employees

ETPs offer basic numeracy and literacy training as well as opportunities to study for National Vocational Qualification (NVQ) Level 2. The pilots give small businesses access to a pot of money to help train their staff and provide compensation for the time their employees take off work to train. So far, nearly 13,000 employers and almost 90,000 employees are benefiting from ETP-funded training. The schemes have been particularly helpful in attracting employees who are traditionally hard to reach – those who left school at 16 with few or no qualifications and have not done any formal learning since.

RAISING THE BAR ON SKILLS DEVELOPMENT

Smart and Kleen Laundries, based in Newcastle, joined an ETP to improve key skills among its workforce. The company took advantage of an ETP run by the Learning and Skills Council in Tyne and Wear that offers employers training subsidies and wage compensation.

Several of Smart and Kleen's staff have received training and support from Newcastle College in literacy and numeracy skills, which will directly help them in their roles as machine operators.

Initially the group expressed doubts about returning to learning, but with regular visits from training assessors they found it was a smooth transition and are now due to take key skills exams in literacy and numeracy.

Brian Moore, managing director, says: "I have been impressed with the ETP scheme. It has boosted staff confidence, which I believe is essential if they're to achieve their potential through training."

---

the union learning fund

Another initiative that gives companies financial support is the Union Learning Fund (ULF), which helps trade unions to use their influence with employers, employees and others to encourage greater take up of learning at work, and to boost their capacity as learning organisations. A key part of the fund is to focus on the partnership between unions and employers, which maximises the contribution of union learning – not only to lifelong learning but also to workforce development.

It now runs 450 courses for workers signed up by shop-floor learning union reps. Education Secretary Charles Clarke says: "Projects have been successful in reaching out to people who have been left out of learning opportunities, such as shift or part-time workers."

skills for life

Skills for Life is the national strategy for improving adult literacy and numeracy skills. Many projects have successfully engaged employers in the issue of addressing skills for life in the workplace. Last year, 8,000 people completed a Basic Skills initial assessment via the ULF, which led to a learning plan. Almost all of the 48 ULF projects in 2003-04 addressed Skills for Life as part of their objectives.

FIRST IN LINE FOR TRAINING

Dave Pugh left school with no qualifications. However, since being elected in 2000 as a trade union representative at First, the UK's largest bus operator, he has completed a range of union courses, attended an Advanced Communication and Tutoring Skills course, and has just completed a Masters Degree in Lifelong Learning at Hull University.

In 2001, when First introduced Lifelong Learning, Dave became one of three union learning representatives, liaising with management and external learning organisations to provide learning opportunities for 1,300 staff at three depots.

He recently won the Learning Representative of the Year award at Leeds College of Technology. In April 2003 he was appointed project co-ordinator for First Group's Yorkshire Division, providing on-site learning centres at 10 depots for 5,000 staff. Through his trade union he is now a part-time tutor at Hull University where he lectures on health and safety and labour law.

The Government's Skills Strategy White Paper, published last year, announced a new entitlement to free tuition for adults who do not have a full Level 2 qualification. The scheme is currently being trialled in two regions. The official target for 2010 is to cut the 6.7m adults in the workforce currently lacking a Level 2 qualification by 40 per cent. In the population as a whole, there are currently 15m adults who lack this level of qualification.

In addition to generic qualifications there are those that have been developed for industry by industry, such as the ITQ, which stands for Information Technology Qualification – as opposed to an IT NVQ – and reflects an individual's IT skills and competence most accurately. This qualification came out of a project initiated by e-skills UK (the Sector Skills Council for the IT industry), the LSC and the Qualifications Curriculum Authority (QCA) to raise the level of IT user skills in the workforce. Employers have warmed to the ITQ, not least because it is a points-based qualification and can pick up other IT qualifications such as the European Computer Driving Licence (ECDL) and Microsoft certification, and consolidate them into the full ITQ.

These basic skills initiatives are designed to help employers tackle the additional problems of employee engagement, particularly where staff with a long-term absence from learning lack the confidence to start again. David Greer says: "The key here is not the content of the training, but the way in which it is delivered. ETPs have been particularly effective at assessing an individual's skills and competence, recognising and crediting them, then comparing them with the national occupational standards of the industry and providing the appropriate training to fill the gap. In this way people are motivated to overcome the barriers."

At this stage it is important for employers to start looking more widely at the skills required at all levels. These can be addressed through a wide range of schemes, including Apprenticeships, programmes aimed at improving technical skills, and NVQ training to Level 3 and above. Employers might also consider vocational qualifications such as BTECs and City & Guilds, both of which are popular, highly respected and used internationally. Sector specific programmes, such as the BIT NVQ, for the automotive sector, provide a more specialised solution to skills shortages. This is covered in more detail in later chapters.

LSC HELP ALREADY IN PLACE

Level 2

The Skills Strategy White Paper announced a new entitlement to free tuition for adults who do not have a full Level 2 qualification and who commit to achieving one. The entitlement is currently being trialled in two regions, the South East and North East.

Apprenticeships

Apprentices learn through a combination of on- and off-the-job education and training. Apprenticeships offer a fantastic range of training in 80 different sectors of industry, covering a huge range of subjects from health and social care to business administration.

Employer Training Pilots (ETPs)

These help employers by offer entitlement to a minimum amount of paid time off during working time, and financial support for employers - to compensate them for providing paid time off. They offer free information, guidance and support for employers and employees taking part in the scheme.

Employer Skills Offer

This scheme will be available through local LSC offices from April 2005. Its primary objective is to engage with and support employers who have not previously invested in workforce skills development, and can access the scheme through a broker, for example a Business Link advisor.

HELP ALREADY IN PLACE

Union Learning Fund

This supports unions in partnership projects to develop work-based learning opportunities for employees. The Fund has helped support and train over 10,000 Union Learning Representatives whose main function is to advise union members about the training and educational development. In turn they have helped over 58,000 people develop new skills or update existing ones, including basic literacy, numeracy, computer skills and continuing professional development.

Other sources of help and information include:

Get On Campaign

A Department for Education and Skills initiative that focuses on the 3.5 million adults who are in work but also have language, literacy or numeracy skills needs.

Sector Skills Councils (SSCs)

These are employer-led and actively involve trade unions, professional bodies and other stakeholders in the sector. to tackle the skills and productivity needs of their sector throughout the UK.

Investors in People (IiP)

The IiP standard is a tried and tested flexible framework that helps companies succeed and compete through improved people performance.

Learndirectbusiness

This offers innovative online learning solutions for organisations of all types and sizes, and works closely with a number of organisations in different sectors of industry. Many of these organisations have linked together to manage dedicated learning centres for businesses and individuals working within that sector.

attracting new talent

There are currently 180 different Apprenticeships available that can provide tailor-made vocational training, says Jane Simms

Apprenticeships can be effective ways to plug skills gaps. Reforms introduced earlier this year will deliver a more flexible Apprenticeship 'ladder of opportunity', beginning at the age of 14 and extending to adults who might have missed out when younger.

They provide 'on the job' training that gives young people the skills their organisations need. The Learning and Skills Council (LSC) funds the cost of the training by providing between £2,500 and £14,000, depending on the sector and the Apprenticeship.

Apprenticeships and Advanced Apprenticeships enable young people aged 16-24, who can be either new or existing employees, to undertake a mixture of on and off-the-job training that will lead to key skills qualifications, a National Vocational Qualification (NVQ) at Level 2 or 3 and the relevant technical certificate.

EXECUTIVE SUMMARY

☐ there is growing recognition that vocational training is as valid a route to employment as academic learning

☐ Apprenticeships take between one and four years to complete depending on the Apprenticeship and level

☐ Some larger companies have their own training schemes that are recognised by the LSC as an Apprenticeship

Since their launch in 1993, Apprenticeships have evolved significantly. In 1994, there were 2,000 apprentices in 14 different skills areas. Now there are over 180 different Apprenticeships in more than 80 sectors of industry and commerce.

SKILLS FOR LIFE

In September BT Retail recruited 300 additional Apprentices covering a wide range of work areas from engineering to HR, as part of its long-term commitment to Apprenticeships. This represents an increase of 76 per cent on last year.

Drawing in young recruits is central to BT's strategy for strengthening its workforce in order to secure a dynamic, motivated and skilled company for the future. A significant proportion of the company's senior management posts are filled by former Apprentices.

Chief executive Pierre Danon says: "Not only does employing Apprentices bring enthusiastic 'can-do' people into our workforce, it also allows us to contribute to our social responsibility towards youth employment. Apprenticeships allow our young people to start on a road of 'learning for life', ensuring they are always ready to meet the needs of our customers."

BT is selective in who it takes on its Apprenticeship scheme, and it offers participants enhanced development opportunities beyond the expected scope of the scheme. In addition to BTEC, Key Skills, HNC/HND or even degree training, additional courses allow them to broaden their knowledge or move to expert status in their chosen field.

Additional craft skills are developed that enable learners to work on higher-level duties, and sometimes to experience junior management responsibilities. And, life skills are enhanced by a range of other development opportunities, including the Prince's Trust, which involves them in the local community and stimulates them to take responsibility for self-advancement.

Dave Haydon, a 23-year-old engineering Apprentice, has found life at BT 'a life-changing experience' after two years in the army. "My Apprenticeship has not only given me the skills to become a customer service engineer, it has also transformed me from a young inexperienced boy into a knowledgeable working adult with a broader outlook and appreciation of people and life in general," he says.

These include IT, accounting and other service areas as well as traditional sectors such as engineering and construction. What's more, there is a growing recognition that vocational training is an equally valid route to employment.

Stephen Gardner, director of work-based learning at the LSC, says: "Apprenticeships offer businesses the means to develop not just the kind of workforce they need today, but to build and protect the workforce they will need in the future.

"By offering Apprenticeships, employers support and create a more efficient, motivated and confident workforce with the skills that directly improve business performance."

The content of each Apprenticeship is decided on by the relevant Sector Skills

Council (SSC) that represents employers' interests. The amount of 'off the job' training differs from sector to sector and employer to employer in order to suit each organisation and individual.

Apprenticeships deliver a range of skills and depend on commitment from apprentice, employer and training provider. This positive 'buy-in' from all parties creates a trustful relationship between the young person and employer that can directly benefit the business through employee retention and the development of industry-specific skills.

signing up

The majority of apprentices are employed directly by their employer who pays them a wage, while receiving financial assistance from the LSC to offset the cost of the Apprenticeship training. The funding received depends on the type of Apprenticeship undertaken, as does the time taken to complete, which varies between one and four years (depending on the sector).

Most small businesses use an external college or training provider to provide the 'off the job' learning element of the Apprenticeship. It is the role of the relevant local LSC office to advise not only on the most suitable Apprenticeship but also on a suitable training provider in the area.

MAKING BEST USE OF APPRENTICESHIPS

- ☐ design a scheme that gives Apprentices the skills that the employer will be able to make use of later on

- ☐ by providing support through the Apprenticeship, monitoring progress and working with the training provider, you can develop the Apprentice to the best of their ability and help meet the needs of the company

- ☐ because Apprentices learn from everyone in the company, many of their 'teachers' are prompted to do further learning, helping to create a learning environment

- ☐ celebrate success. Many companies have Apprentice Awards Events, which can be extended into staff awards, again helping to foster a learning culture

- ☐ share best practice with other employers who also offer Apprenticeships.

FOOD FOR THOUGHT

"It's not the cost of training employees that counts, but the cost of not training them," says Steven Bell, chief executive of Bells Stores, the North East's leading convenience chain. The company, now part of the Sainsburys Group, is planning to increase the number of stores from 54 to 80, meaning that investment in staff has never been more crucial.

Bells Stores has been involved in vocational training for over two decades. Through a standalone training company – Bells Training Services – the company delivers Apprenticeships and many other work-based learning programmes as part of its ethos of 'matching people to expansion'.

"We believe passionately that Apprenticeships raises our professional standards, supports our expansion plans and improves profitability," says Bell. The company was also one of the first food retailers to be awarded Investors in People (IiP) in 1992.

Bells has a flat management structure that offers job security and promotion opportunities from within, and many of its employees become managers young. Having such motivated staff allows Bells to live its strap line: 'More enthusiasm per square foot' – a claim borne out by the fact that customers visit their stores more frequently and spend more with them per year than any other North East food retailer.

TRAINING IN TOP GEAR

In keeping with its premium brand, BMW takes its responsibility to provide quality training very seriously. Adrian Davies, BMW's career strategies manager, says: "Our Apprenticeships are integral to the continued success of BMW, so it's imperative that they're equipped with the highest possible skills," he says.

Over recent years, BMW's 18-year-old Apprenticeship scheme has evolved significantly. Three years ago the company moved all its training inhouse in order to make best use of all the knowledge within the company, and built a 2,500 square foot training centre in Bracknell, which is expected to almost double in size in the near future.

Equipped with modern facilities, the centre boasts new lecture rooms, workshops with the latest fibre optic technology, a fleet of 12 cars for dedicated use by Apprentices, and luxury off-site campus accommodation. New Apprentices are inducted to the company through an outward bound course in Dartmoor – one of many examples of the company's determination to set new precedents in the quality of Apprenticeships offered.

As part of the programme, Apprentices cover units on body shop and servicing, technical and mechanical engineering, health and safety and key skills. But the development of Apprentices goes beyond this learning, explains Davies. "We regard every Apprentice as a valid team member. We strive to teach them how to think for themselves, use their initiative and explore all the issues. "

While the motor industry as a whole suffers from poor retention of Apprentices (around half leave during or after training), 97 per cent of BMW's Apprentices go on to enjoy successful careers within the company. The programme also attracts more applicants, and BMW's intake is 20 per cent higher, than those of its competitors.

The success of former BMW Apprentices is testimony to the quality of their training. For example, one is now a member of the team responsible for developing and implementing the training course he began on, while another went on to work for a Formula 1 racing team.

trouble at the top?

Leadership has been identified as a key skills gap in companies. Jane Simms outlines a number of initiatives and programmes that address this

Numerous surveys attest to the dearth of high-quality management and leadership skills in the UK. This is to UK companies' cost. Research conducted by Demos for the Chartered Management Institute confirmed a strong relationship between the systematic implementation of leadership development and organisational performance.

owner-managers neglect their own skills needs

The research revealed that small firms, who arguably have most to gain from developing more professional leaders and managers, are the least likely to do so. Owner-managers, however good they are at providing training for their staff, often neglect to invest in their own skills, believing that academic qualifications or on-the-job experience equip them to run a business. They often think they're too busy to develop themselves, making the common mistake of believing that leadership is innate and cannot be developed through learning.

EXECUTIVE SUMMARY

☐ in 2003, the Council for Excellence in Leadership and Management reported on the lack of financial support available for leaders and managers within the 20-250 employee bracket

☐ another problem was the absence of an effective business support network

☐ in response, the Learning and Skills Council launched its Leadership and Management Programme

As part of the Government's Skills Strategy, the Council for Excellence in Leadership and Management produced a report last year setting out recommendations for addressing the management and leadership challenge. One of the problems

RESTRUCTURING FOR STRATEGIC SUCCESS

Systems ADI Group acts as a one-stop engineering solutions shop for customers in the manufacturing industry. The group has grown organically since it was established 15 years ago. Most of its 23 managers have come up from the shop floor and have no management training.

The business plans to increase its turnover from £10m to £40m over the next five years, but knows that it cannot achieve its target without training its managers to carry out active front-line roles in the expanding organisation.

With the help of Business Link, Systems ADI developed a new structure to match its new business plan. Using behavioural profiling, it identified how its managers would fit into that structure and what development needs they had in order to fulfil their own ambitions and contribute to the business's overall strategy.

The cost of the management assessment, behavioural profiling, management training and creating personal development plans for all 23 managers amounted to £25,000 over two years. This was funded 60 per cent by the company and 40 per cent by the LSC through Business Link.

On the recommendation of the Business Link adviser all Systems ADI managers have just embarked on an NVQ Level 3 management course at Bourneville Business School in Birmingham. The course has been tailored to the company's particular needs and approved by the Chartered Management Institute,.

Alan Lusty, managing director of Systems ADI Group, is attending the course with his fellow directors. "I have no qualifications whatsoever, and there is clearly lots I can learn," he says. "Besides, I want to show solidarity with my managers."

The company is already reaping benefits, says Lusty. "Our managers are motivated by our commitment to developing them, and their leadership and management training is helping them to cope with the big new pressures we have put on them."

---

it identified was the lack of financial support available for leaders and managers within the 20–250 employee bracket. Another potentially more serious problem was the absence of an effective business support network to signpost organisations and individuals to a solution best suited to their particular needs.

Organisations have responded with a variety of initiatives. For example, the Learning and Skills Council has launched its Leadership and Management Programme, which makes available up to £1,000 for skills assessments and training to directors of businesses employing 20-250 employees.

KEY LEADERSHIP SKILLS

- [ ] having a clear vision or sense of purpose and the ability to communicate that in a way such that everyone can see they are making a difference
- [ ] the ability to listen. This is possibly the least utilised leadership skill, and more so the higher up the organisation you go. It's about taking time with teams, with individuals and large groups, and being seen to seek feedback and ideas and act on them
- [ ] leading by example, and putting into practice the things you talk about such as matching behaviours with your mission statement. It's no good claiming you have an 'open door' policy and then sitting in your office with your door closed working on a backlog of emails
- [ ] developing a leadership culture within the organisation

The focus of the Leadership and Management programme is on building very strong networks between Business Links and a range of intermediaries including accountants, bank managers, professional associations and other businesses. The aim is to get them to engage with SMEs in order to identify where the skills gaps are. They can then direct them to the appropriate place to find help.

Keith Bartlett, LSC skills policy manager, says: "Management skills play a vital role during the setting up and growth period of a company. If these skills are not nurtured, a company's future performance is put under threat.

By developing and funding a programme which identifies the skills needs of directors and provides tailored training, the LSC is helping to improve the decision-making skills and strategic thinking of England's managers."

diagnosing leadership and management needs

The programme takes a managing director or other key decision-maker through a diagnostic process to determine their leadership and management needs, helps them draw up a development plan and reimburses them for up to £1,000 of any development activities they undertake in order to carry out their plan. These activities are not necessarily formal. For example, the director might go and spend the day in a another organisation, join a professional body, get a coach or mentor in addition to, or instead, of enrolling on courses or gaining qualifications.

SELF-DIRECTED LEARNING

Vestas Blades UK is a blade research, development and manufacturing company. In 2002, it set itself some stretching goals, including reducing manufacturing times and costs, introducing 24-hour, seven-day production, launching three new blade designs and increasing quality and reliability.

The company saw learning as playing a key role in developing its capability to achieve its strategic objectives. It wanted the learning to be continuous, timely and relevant, and both motivating for employees and able to meet the needs of the business. The decision was made to use Self-Directed Learning (SDL) groups as a means to this end.

Twenty managers piloted the SDL programme, which kicked off by helping participants identify their own learning needs in order to achieve the kind of performance required to meet the business's strategic and operational objectives. They were then made aware of the wealth of learning resources available through books and e-learning, and were put into groups of four who met every six weeks to provide vital mutual support and get guidance from a facilitator.

Each group had its own facilitator who helped each member to:

☐ articulate clearly the issues they saw as important to their progress

☐ focus more on what is within their sphere of influence and control and less on what is not

☐ identify how their attitudes and subsequent behaviours contribute to successes and difficulties

☐ gauge emotions, ask insightful questions and listen actively

☐ give and receive feedback

☐ use colleagues to achieve specific objectives, for instance, as role players to act out a group or one-to-one meeting by way of preparation for one which was due to take place

Vestas believes the SDL learning programme has helped the vast majority of home-grown talent cope with the demands of leadership, and it achieved exceptional results by achieving its strategic objectives.

SDL has become an integral part of the culture and learning is seen as an important part of the psychological contract Vestas has with its staff.

The LSC hopes that leaders and managers involved in the programme will recognise the importance of workforce development as a fundamental building block of high performance and consequently make changes to their organisation's culture – cascading training and development down through the organisation. This is important says Ian Lawson, chief executive of the Campaign for

---

OTHER LEADERSHIP DEVELOPMENT TOOLS

- [ ] the Investors in People (IiP) Leadership and Management model helps organisations assess leadership and management capacity in some depth

- [ ] the Management Standards Centre has just finished developing new world-class occupational standards for leadership and management

- [ ] the Campaign for Leadership at the Work Foundation has a leadership profiling tool called Liberating Leadership, which allows managers to rate themselves against how their teams perceive them, leading to better dialogue and change

- [ ] the Chartered Management Institute offers the chartered manager qualification, which builds management and leadership skills through a reflective and developmental process

- [ ] the Chartered Institute of Personnel Development is promoting self-directed learning (SDL) as a way of building leadership expertise. For more information, go to www.cipd.co.uk\helpingpeoplelearn

---

Leadership at the Work Foundation, because the need for leaderships skills throughout the organisation is increasingly being recognised. "Being a leader is not about being a charismatic figurehead, but about creating a leadership organisation," he says. "The way to judge a good leader is on results, how they get them and, crucially, what happens when they are not there."

ap association of learning providers

Working with government, employers and providers to skill the nation:

Representing the employers and learning providers that use Government funds to deliver vocational skills at the workplace.

Ensuring that the capacity of learning providers and employers are properly accessed and fully used in developing the skills the economy needs.

Over the past two years ALP has more than trebled its membership, growing and evolving into a powerful and respected voice in the vocational learning sector.

Join us in influencing the development of the National Skills Strategy from an employer/provider perspective.

Visit us at www.learningproviders.org.uk

ap association of learning providers

measuring progress

Monitoring the effectiveness of your training investment on a regular basis is a must, says Philip Hunter

There is abundant evidence that skills shortages lead to lower productivity and profitability within all business sectors as well as for individual companies. In 2003, the Learning and Skills Council (LSC) surveyed 72,000 employers, and discovered that 135,000 vacancies in England – 20 per cent of the total – remained unfilled directly through a lack of skilled applicants.

training does pay

The implication that companies could improve their bottom line if they invested in training seems obvious, but absolute proof is still lacking. However, there is some evidence that training does pay, not least from a recent study carried out for Investors in People (IiP) UK, a public body funded by the Department for Education and Skills to develop and promote a framework for workforce development.

The study looked at 22 companies who work with the IiP standard to align training and development of their workforce with the

EXECUTIVE SUMMARY

- [ ] many companies do not know how to evaluate the success of their training investment
- [ ] companies that make training integral to their ethos and business processes gain the most from it
- [ ] not everyone is best suited to theory based learning. Finding out if employees have preferred methods of training is useful
- [ ] a workforce development broker can help identify which courses and methods are most appropriate

business strategy, adopting an 'assess, train, assess', approach. These companies were invited to use the DTI's best practice diagnostic tool, Benchmark Plus (www.dti.gov.uk/implementbestpractice/benchmarking.html). This tool allows a company to compare all its business practices, processes and outcomes against those of its peers.

About two thirds of these companies – 15 in total – were shown to be more profitable than peer companies who had previously used the benchmark index (using a pre-tax profit as a percentage of turnover as the measure of profitability). Although only a small study, the message is that businesses are most likely to gain from training when it is embedded within their ethos and processes, rather than just obtained on an adhoc basis to meet specific needs.

a sustained commitment

Without a doubt, there will always be a place for reactive training to meet a specific need that crops up, perhaps during a particular project or as the result of acquiring a new customer. There might be a need to train staff in a new computer package, for example, and the justification for this is easy to make because if the training is not done the particular project cannot be under-taken. But it is the ongoing proactive training, for example, in negotiating skills or personnel management, which is harder to quantify. For this reason the IiP study breaks new ground by demonstrating that firms can benefit from an ongoing commitment to training.

Yet while many businesses are now convinced of the general need for training they remain unsure as to how to assess the value of different components and determine what is the best way forward. This was clear from the responses captured by the LSC National Employers Skills Survey to questions based on 10 key employer engagement indicators (see box on opposite page).

These indicators were designed to measure the extent to which companies engage in the kind of plan-implement-review approach to training, which ensures that training spend is an investment, and is not just a cost. The findings of this survey highlighted wide variations between companies and sectors, reflecting varying approaches and attitudes to the value of training.

THE PLAN-IMPLEMENT-REVIEW PROCESS

Ten questions to ask yourself when considering training and development in your organisation are:

☐ do we have a business plan?

☐ do we have a training plan?

☐ do we have a budget for training?

☐ how much did we spend per employee last year on training and development?

☐ how many of our employees have received training in the last year?

☐ how many of our employees have an annual performance review?

☐ do all our employees have a job description?

☐ have we assessed the skills gaps in our organisation?

☐ do we assess the training we provide and the trainees?

evaluating your training

Guidance on how to measure training is now available from a variety of sources, such as the Business Link website (www.businesslink.gov.uk) which includes a section called Evaluate your Training. This sets out six key benefits obtained by training evaluation (see box on page 58), and recommends the Kirkpatrick model for companies that want to evaluate training themselves, under the four headings of Reaction, Learning, Behaviour and Results. These generate both qualitative and quantitative data taken before during and after courses with the ultimate aim being to assess how the performance and behaviour of staff has changed.

Business Link also advocates evaluation of different training methods. The most common ones are:

☐ self study

☐ one-to-one coaching

☐ group learning in classes

☐ work-based assignments

BENCHMARKING PROGRESS

Many companies know that investment in skills pays even if they cannot prove it, but would still like some measure of the benefits if only to target their training effort more effectively. Clamason Industries, a west Midlands manufacturer, is one such company.

The firm, which makes pressed metal parts for a wide range of products from computer housings to boilers, is in a highly competitive international market where it cannot compete on labour costs. It must therefore maximise quality and added value while also maintaining tight budget control. This requires a range of skills within its relatively small workforce of 110, with training given to almost all staff.

Recently the company took the chance to assess the value of its training against the DTI's Benchmark Index, designed to compare performance against competitors in its industry sector across a range of about 80 indicators in areas such as material and labour costs, inventory, customer satisfaction, quality, and job satisfaction.

Clamason was one of 22 companies chosen to take part in a survey by the DTI and Investors in People (IiP) UK on the impact of skills development on business performance.

The results were clear cut, with significant benefits recorded in each of five performance categories, which can be summarised as:

- budgetary control
- profit/value per employee
- quality and customer satisfaction
- supply chain optimisation
- and staff satisfaction

Skills were taught under each of these categories, and the impact measured.

budgetary control
The financial director ran courses to make supervisors more aware of issues in budgeting control so that they could then take responsibility for it. As a result expenditure was reduced by 50 per cent and working capital by 60 per cent.

profit/value per employee
Supervisors were sent on workshops at Wolverhampton University on modern techniques such as lean manufacturing designed to streamline materials flow on production lines to maximise output and reduce stock levels.

Targets were then set for staff appraisals. As a result, direct costs including both labour and materials were cut, and the company rose into the DTI Benchmark's top quartile in its sector for both value added and turnover per employee.

BENCHMARKING PROGRESS

quality and customer satisfaction

Operatives were trained in quality inspection and to handle different work schedules and processes. This meant that quality problems were usually trapped inhouse before customers noticed, and the workforce flexibility made it easier to meet changing customer demands. The bottom line was then that customer satisfaction climbed into the DTI Benchmark's top quartile.

supply chain optimisation

Staff were trained in supply chain management tools and techniques. Buyers of materials were trained in consignment and inventory management. This led to a reduction of 20 per cent in inventory and a 10 per cent improvement in stock turn. The latter is a measure of how often the company's stock of products that are ready for customers is replaced within a given period. Costs are reduced by having a high stock turn because fewer products then have to be stored before being delivered to customers. Clamason is also reducing the number of suppliers it uses, which in turn saves money on administration and makes it easier to negotiate good prices. Taken together these supply chain 'tuning' measures have significantly reduced costs.

job satisfaction

Several initiatives have been aimed at staff motivation, retention, and safety. Health and safety training is given on induction to new employees and to existing staff in refresher courses. Team leaders are trained in how to manage disciplinary and staff grievance procedures, and also in how to deal with staff absenting themselves without leave. Results noted in the DTI Benchmarks include significant reductions in absenteeism and in accidents, and rating in the top quartile on all staff satisfaction measures.

- [ ] external courses

- [ ] e-learning

Each of these methods has pros and cons that need to be considered in the context of differing requirements of the company and the individual. Often a company will combine several of these. There is also a fundamental choice between in-house and external training. The latter can provide greater access to best practices and, while more expensive at the point of delivery, avoids the need to maintain specialist training skills in-house. On the other hand, external courses can fail to match the business needs, and this can be identified through proper evaluation. Yet employers are sometimes guilty of accepting whatever external training courses are most readily available, rather than taking the time

SIX GOOD REASONS FOR EVALUATING TRAINING

☐ tracks development of staff knowledge and skills

☐ finds out if learning is being applied in the workplace

☐ identifies current training gaps and future training needs

☐ establishes if the money you invested in training was worth it

☐ informs future training plans and strategy

☐ ensures training continually improves

Source: Businesslink

to identify which ones will best match their requirements, or working with training providers to tailor courses to their needs.

using a training broker

For SMEs the task of sifting through the different options can be daunting and, in practice, it is usually impossible to evaluate them all firsthand. For this reason, the LSC recommends that businesses consider using a broker to help identify methods and individual courses on offer. This enables a business to side step some of the evaluation process, although it will still be necessary to monitor the courses and assess their contribution to skills and profitability.

To ensure that your business gets value from its investment in training, it is important to monitor courses or programmes using measurable criteria and set learning objectives. Gut instinct is not always the best gauge of success. Specific objectives that can be set include:

☐ improved sales

☐ reduced cost per sale

☐ better employee performance

☐ reduced staff turnover

☐ improved morale, eg reduced absenteeism, greater contribution through new ideas

☐ fewer customer complaints

- ☐ positive feedback from staff about value of training
- ☐ greater innovation

Any of these measures, may not relate directly to training if taken in isolation. However, taken together they provide a useful goal to aim for while at the same time providing data of use in assessing the progress, or lack of it, made so far.

Measuring the impact of training is of little use without corresponding action being taken to improve its efficacy. Such improvements are likely to come first through gearing training more closely to overall business objectives, and then in tuning it in to the needs of individual employees.

the need for a business plan

All too often, training is not matched to business needs. This is particularly true when the business is undergoing change, prompting the need for new skills. This is why one of the 10 questions on the LSC's skills survey asked whether companies had a business plan. In several sectors barely more than half the companies had a business plan at all, and in construction it was 41 per cent. The number of companies within each sector with a training plan is lower still.

Yet there is plenty of evidence that a training plan yields measurable benefits. This is particularly obvious in the case of apprenticeship schemes designed to provide a renewable source of skills vital for a company's success (see chapter 7).

The success of such schemes is relatively easy to measure in terms such as how many of the apprentices remain with the business, and what contribution they make.

There is a cost in terms of in-house commitment from experienced staff, and usually also in external courses as part of the apprenticeship. However, these can be measured against the benefits of having the training tailored to the company's needs, and the ability to adapt it to the emerging requirements of the trainees. It may be that some trainees require more help with one aspect of their apprenticeship and less with another.

Indeed, training in general is more effective if it meets both the skills needs of the employer and the personality and learning habits of the employee. Some people, for example, are not good at absorbing knowledge from books but are quick on the uptake and able to learn on the job. For them job shadowing – working alongside someone experienced in a particular task – may prove most effective.

assessment must be continual

The overall message is that accurate assessment on an ongoing basis is imperative. Without it, it's impossible to deliver a flexible training strategy that matches the needs of both business and staff, as there is no way of telling whether particular approaches or courses are working or failing.

giving as well as receiving

Companies need to forge closer links with local training providers. Those that already have are reaping the benefits, says Philip Hunter

Company directors often complain that training courses, colleges and other providers fail to instil relevant skills in their students. One direct way to address this is for directors to get involved with local colleges and training providers, and influencing the direction and content of relevant courses.

In 2002, the IoD conducted a survey of 244 members which revealed that 60 per cent of directors were involved with secondary schools. Fifty two per cent of respondents had links with a higher education institution and almost two-fifths (39 per cent), were connected with an FE college.

Almost a quarter of directors responding to the survey (23 per cent) were members of a school or further education college governing body.

EXECUTIVE SUMMARY

☐ engaging with colleges and independent providers is the best way for businesses to signal what their specific training needs are

☐ too often in the past, FE colleges and providers have offered courses on a take-it-or-leave-it basis

☐ colleges can also act as training brokers for companies

☐ directors will often improve their own management skills when giving support to local colleges

A further IoD survey, carried out in May 2004 that specifically addressed members' links with colleges showed that 12 per cent of the 141 directors polled had used a college Business Development Unit for customised training or consultancy services, and 17 per cent had had input into the development of courses provided by a local college.

BENEFITS OF ENGAGEMENT

The potential benefits for businesses of working with local training providers include:

- ☐ influencing overall direction towards more market led approach to course development
- ☐ making courses more relevant to immediate needs
- ☐ obtaining feedback from colleges, providers and other companies in area on best practices in governance
- ☐ discovering what grants might be available towards training your staff
- ☐ finding out where the best or most appropriate courses are, even if your college or local provider do not offer them

While the benefits of participation in training for UK plc as a whole are beyond dispute, some directors have difficulty identifying the immediate benefits for their own companies given that it can take a significant investment of time and effort. Yet few that have taken the trouble to involve themselves with say their local college regret the effort. According to Professor Mike Campbell, director of strategy and research for the SSDA (Sector Skills Development Agency), the hard part is persuading companies to take the first step. Once communication with the local training provider has been made, companies' involvement usually deepens.

Some fledgling companies won't have the time or need to engage with their local college. But, according to Campbell, most such companies reach a point in their life-cycle when they become aware of a particular skills shortage and feel the need to take some longer-term action to address this within their own area or sector. This can also occur within long-established companies when, for example, they launch a new product or face changing competitive pressure. Rolls Royce decided to help set up a local Centre of Vocational Excellence to provide skills within the Derby area in lean manufacturing to cut its production costs (see case study).

taking a longer term view

In some instances directors have to be persuaded to take a longer strategic view, to make that first commitment to a local college or training community. In the case of Rolls Royce, there was no immediate pay back, but there are tangible benefits. These can extend beyond having an influence on the development and content of courses. The experience of Michael Davis, managing director of the Centre of Enterprise, Leicester, a non-profit making organisation administering the Learning and Skills Council's training programme in the area, for example, suggests that directors can improve their own management skills by becoming involved closely with a local college. They can exchange knowledge with other directors, and also learn more about corporate governance. Davis is also a governor of Leicester College, which is a bigger organisation than the Centre of Enterprise and he is therefore learning how to cope with management problems on a different scale. Davis has gained expertise in general financial procedures, risk management, and overall corporate governance. Such close relationships with a local college or provider will almost always be symbiotic rather than purely altruistic on the part of company directors.

Nevertheless, perhaps the greatest benefit is in helping colleges and providers to understand what the real training requirements are locally and ensuring that their courses evolve accordingly. It's not only companies that need to change their mindset. Colleges could also do a lot more to encourage local businesses to get involved, and not just with management, but also course development.

Traditionally, menus of courses have been offered by colleges and providers almost on a take-it-or-leave-it basis. The challenge now is for these to become more market driven, treating local businesses as customers. This means providing products, ie. courses, that customers want to buy, which means they must be relevant and offer good value for money. Colleges and providers can only find out what businesses want through engagement.

giving the right signals

By the same token it's unrealistic for companies to expect their local colleges and providers to tune course programmes to the skills they require if they fail to provide them with the in-depth knowledge of their business. Companies must give the right signals. It is then up to the colleges to interpret and translate these signals into appropriate courses with associated qualifications at the given level.

While local colleges and providers may not be able to meet all the requirements of businesses in their area, they can act as honest brokers to help find the right

FINE-TUNING MANUFACTURING SKILLS

Centres of Vocational Excellence (CoVEs) are being created as part of a major government initiative to address the chronic shortage of people with intermediate skills based around NVQ Level 3 by strengthening the links between employers and local FE colleges and providers.

The five-year £240m programme runs to March 2006, aiming to create 400 individual centres dedicated to specific skills relevant to their region or locality, or to a given industry sector. By September 2004 there were 260 CoVEs.

A good example of one that addresses local needs for specific skills is the joint venture between Rolls Royce, Derby College and the Learning and Skills Council (LSE). Derby has a high concentration of engineering companies such as Rolls Royce.

The CoVE in Derby provides training specifically in lean manufacturing techniques designed to identify and eliminate waste in the production process, thereby reducing costs and avoiding unnecessary consumption of floor space. Since lean manufacturing is a relatively new process the skills it requires are often in short supply. According to Rolls Royce, it boils down to about six key principles, which are now being taught to 200 people a week, from 14 years old upwards, including GCSE students and Rolls Royce apprentices who follow Derby College's programme.

The CoVE fulfils the equally important role of engaging employers in the area, and will be introducing short courses for other engineering companies in lean manufacturing techniques. This will also give directors and managers of engineering companies in the area the chance to provide feedback on course content, developing the two-way communication process between providers and consumers of training that is vital to make it more relevant to employers' needs.

courses. This can be difficult for a company on its own, and a relationship with the local college or provider can be invaluable in sifting through the options and finding the closest match to a particular need.

Employers may also be able to discover how to apply for grants towards the cost of training their staff. Such grants are available from a variety of sources, including local, national and European agencies (see chapter 6), and many companies fail to take them up through ignorance or reluctance to negotiate the bureaucratic minefields involved.

Employers can also influence the strategic direction of training and skills development at a higher level through the Sector Skills Councils (www.ssda.org.uk). These are independent UK-wide organisations, led by employers but also involving trade unions and various professional bodies, that shape the course of skills provision in their sector (see chapter 5). This may not be so appealing for smaller companies, but does provide a more direct route of influence into government policy-making.

If there is an overall message for smaller companies in particular, it is that engagement provides a double bonus for employers – long-term influencing of training providers and the potential for valuable knowledge about financial management and corporate governance.

where do we go from here?

Between them, the government and UK business are starting to tackle the skills shortage crisis. Alison Coleman highlights recent achievements and asks what skills will we need for the future?

Skills shortages and gaps have been the bugbear of UK industry for many years. Achieving long-term sustainable solutions to the problem will take many more. However, progress is being made and employers should be heartened by the positive impact already being made by the various programmes and initiatives that have set out to address the skills issue at all levels.

EXECUTIVE SUMMARY

- ☐ as the UK moves towards a value-added, skills-based economy, both individuals and employers will be faced with new challenges
- ☐ business is already benefiting from a raft of government skills improvement initiatives that are underway
- ☐ businesses are being asked to get more involved in the development of new skills initiatives

Throughout 2003/04 colleges and training providers have expanded the flow of adults and young people gaining skills, training and qualifications, with excellent results:

- ☐ basic skill: 200,000 learners achieved at least one qualification in literacy, numeracy or language this year

- ☐ Level 2: a quarter of a million more adults in the workforce achieved qualifications to full Level 2, bringing the proportion of adult workers qualified to that level to 71 per cent

- ☐ Apprenticeships: a quarter of a million people aged between 16 and 24 were enrolled on apprenticeship programmes by the end of March 2004. The programme has had over one million entrants to date

☐ foundation degrees: currently 25,000 students are enrolled on foundation degree courses, with employers involved both in the design and delivery

Problems do, of course, remain. Too few young people gain mastery of the basic skills by the time they leave full time education, with only just over half achieving five or more GCSEs at grades A*-C, whilst completion rates in Apprenticeships are unacceptably low. Sustained effort will be required to correct such deficiencies.

government aims

The government's Skills Strategy, launched in July 2003, set out a clear picture of the skills challenge and how it would be met. Its aim is to strengthen the UK's position as one of the world's leading economies by ensuring that employers have the skills to support the success of their business, and that employees have the necessary skills to be both employable and personally fulfilled. A year on, some businesses are beginning to see benefits, although there is still much work to be done in improving overall educational standards.

Good progress is also also being made in the setting up of the Skills for Business network, with 25 Sector Skills Councils (SSCs) likely to be established by mid 2005. Sector Skills Councils are independent, UK-wide organisations developed by groups of influential employers in industry or business sectors of economic or strategic significance. SSCs are employer-led and actively involve trade unions, professional bodies and other stakeholders in the sector and are licensed by the Secretary of State for Education and Skills, in consultation with Ministers in Scotland, Wales and Northern Ireland, to tackle the skills and productivity needs of their sector throughout the UK.

SSCs give responsibility to employers to provide leadership for strategic action to meet their sector's skills and business needs. In return they receive substantial public investment and greater dialogue with government departments across the UK. This will enable sector employers to have a far greater impact on policies affecting skills and productivity, and increased influence with education and training partners.

At the time of writing, 12 councils have been licensed and three more recommended for licence. Together with the remaining Trailblazer Councils, this will mean that almost half of the workforce is represented.

Reform of the business support network is also well underway. The new Businesslink website (www.businesslink.gov.uk) was successfully launched in May 2004 and is aimed at owners and managers in small to medium-sized enterprises in particular. The website brings together the full range of government information and advice and support tools – including a training directory with over 500,000 courses – to help new and existing enterprises.

promoting innovation

The government's Innovation Strategy, led by the Department of Trade & Industry (DTI) now incorporates skills development as an integral part of promoting innovation. This year saw the launch of the DTI's full new suite of Business Support products.

The LSC has launched a new leadership and management programme aimed at managing directors of SMEs. The programme focuses on supporting informal learning and coaching tailored to meet manager's needs.

a champion programme

Investors in People UK (liP) has developed a Champions programme to recognise and reward liP organisations that actively spread good practice. The programme rewards those businesses that have been outstanding in promoting the values and principles of Investors in People and are sharing good practice with others outside their own organisation.

Organisations undergo a selection process and are awarded Champions status for up to three years, along with a logo and national publicity.

The first Champions were announced by Charles Clarke at the Skills Strategy: One Year On event in July 2004. Sixteen organisations chosen from 246 entrants were awarded Champion status.

The progress made in the last year alone reflects the efforts of the various organisations committed to ensuring that the UK has the skills it needs to sustain industry growth and competitive edge.

THE PROFIT FROM LEARNING PROGRAMME

In 2003 the LSC launched the second phase of its Employer Training Pilots, locally marketed in Essex, East London and Kent as the Profit From Learning (PfL) programme. It enables businesses to up-skill their workforces at basic and intermediate levels through quality training that leads to recognised qualifications. Tailored packages in areas such as manufacturing, retail operations, the care sector, and hospitality and catering have won praise from employers.

Eaden Lilley, a family-owned department store based in Saffron Waldren has benefited from the scheme. Joan Le Fever, the company's store manager, says: "We have nine or 10 people from all departments who are now taking part in the PfL programme and it has been fantastic for the staff. It's given our older staff members the chance to do NVQ Level 2. For many of them this is their first qualification since leaving school."

The training has covered important retail issues, such as security, which has given staff the confidence to deal with situations as they arise. The company is now looking to extend the PfL training sessions throughout the store.

But there is a great deal that businesses can do in order to ensure that current momentum continues. Increasingly they are being asked to play a more active part in the development of new skills initiatives. The new Foundation Degree programme, launched in 2001, is a two-year higher education qualification designed to give people the intermediate technical and professional skills demanded by employers, and to provide more flexible ways of studying. It is employers who have been closely involved in the development and delivery of these programmes.

Businesses must also look ahead to what skills they will need in the future. Globalisation – in particular, the rapid pace of development among European countries – technological advances and changing marketplaces will impact on their requirements. Their skills strategies must reflect this.

challenges for the future

As Digby Jones, director general of the CBI said recently: "Without the right skills, individuals will find life increasingly tough as the UK restructures itself into a value-added, skills-based economy. The challenge now is to deliver what business needs: new management skills in SMEs through Investors in People, more employable young people trained in the most relevant areas, a highly skilled workforce of literate and numerate employees and better quality education and training provision."

The transformation of learning in this country is vital to ensure it is relevant to employers. This will only be achieved if employers themselves are driving the changes needed. A number of LSC initiatives have already started the process, working with employers to demonstrate how they can help to change the system. However, this is a massive task and requires serious commitment, not only from the LSC, but also from employers and learning providers.

Taking this approach means training must respond to a specific employer need or skill gap and be delivered in a way that fits with the needs of the business – at the right time and in the right place, often outside the traditional office hours of 9-5. The employer should feel very much in the driving seat, being able to influence the training to get exactly what they need to make a difference to the bottom line.

The LSC is strengthening and developing its relationship with employers by taking time to talk to employers and those representing them, and speaking the language of business to start the reform of skills and workforce development.

Using skills research and analysis the LSC is able to give direction to business, engaging more employers in shaping policies. We can begin to raise awareness of qualifications and funding available to tackle fundamental skills issues such as poor literacy and numeracy in the adult workforce.

Transforming the learning system to meet demand is key to unlocking the productivity increases needed to match and pass our economic competitors. The LSC has already started to embrace its responsibility in this process.

However, we need both public and private sector spending to be well spent if we are to make serious inroads into the skills deficiencies experienced across the economy. Making learning truly demand-led would be a major achievement with a direct and lasting impact on our economy and future prosperity. It is a difficult journey, but is vital if we are to succeed as a high skill-based, globally competitive economy.